This Book Belongs to:

The Literary Adventures of
Washington Irving

AMERICAN STORYTELLER

written and illustrated by

CHERYL HARNESS

NATIONAL GEOGRAPHIC
WASHINGTON· D·C·

Washington Irving

Sub sole sub umbra Virens

The Irving family motto: *Flourishing in the sun and in the shade*

A Note from the Author

In 1789, when George Washington became the first president, he met many of his fellow Americans, including the subject of this book. Like almost every other president since then, GW had a lot on his mind and he probably forgot all about meeting six-year-old Washington Irving. But then, how was he to know that the pint-sized New Yorker would grow up to be one of his biographers and one of America's most famous storytellers?

As a writer, Washington Irving created the funny, tragic, and spooky story of Rip Van Winkle. He sent a deeply creepy headless horseman galloping through Sleepy Hollow and into our nightmares and movie theaters. His writings about "good St. Nicholas" and old holiday traditions affect our festive ways of Christmas-keeping to this day. As a traveler in America and Europe, he encountered other presidents as well as kings, queens, artists, Barbary pirates, Osage Indians, and Oklahoma bison. As a diplomat, he represented the young United States in Great Britain and Spain. And always, wherever he went, he exercised his twin talents of writing and making friends. When the genial traveler finally settled down, he created a home so beautiful that tourists came to see it back in the 19th century and they still do. All of these things make Washington Irving, literary adventurer, a colorful and exciting American to know.

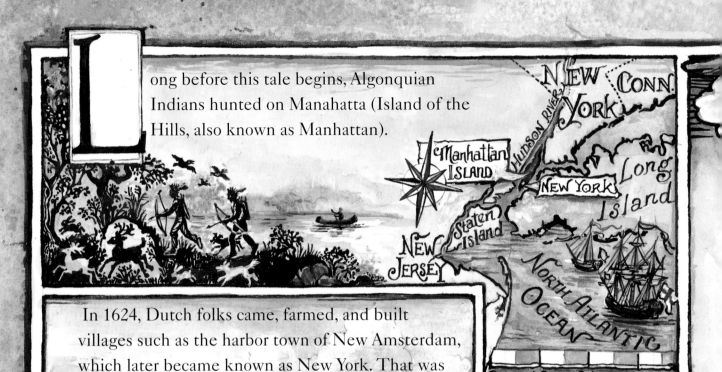

ong before this tale begins, Algonquian Indians hunted on Manahatta (Island of the Hills, also known as Manhattan).

In 1624, Dutch folks came, farmed, and built villages such as the harbor town of New Amsterdam, which later became known as New York. That was after British folks took over in 1664.

Come forward in time to a bright, late fall day, November 25,1783. Great Britain had lost her American colonies in a long, cruel war. Glum British soldiers and civilians were clearing out just as victorious, newly independent Americans were parading into a town noisy with patriotic triumph and aflutter with homemade striped-and-starry banners.

Among the joyful, war-weary New Yorkers that day were William and Sarah Irving and their children: William, Jr. (17), Ann, a.k.a. "Nancy" (13), Peter (11), Catharine (9), Ebenezer (7), John (5), Sally (3), and baby Washington Irving, born on April 3, 1783. His parents named him after General George Washington, the steadfast hero of the American Revolution.

WILLIAM, JR. • WILLIAM and SARAH • PETER •
ANN a.k.a. NANCY • CATHARINE • WASHINGTON • The IRVING Family • SARAH a.k.a. SALLY • EBENEZER • JOHN

The Irving Family

Young Washington grew up in a house at No. 128 William Street, not far from his father's store at No. 75. Mr. Irving sold hardware and other goods that he'd imported from overseas. As the youngest of a big, close family, loads of attention came Washington's way. His formal education began at a neighbor lady's nursery school. Then, in 1789, when he was six, he transferred to a nearby private school. New York City was the nation's capital then, and it wasn't unusual for New Yorkers to catch glimpses of their tall, dignified first president. Lizzie, a Scotswoman who worked in the Irvings' household, was out walking with six-year-old Washington when she spotted the great man going into a shop. Excited Lizzie lost no time following him inside. "Please your Honor," she said, "here's a bairn (child) was named after you."

The "bairn" looked up, up, up into the calm, deep-set eyes of President George Washington, who put his hand on little Washington's dark, curly head.

What did the young lad do for fun?

Washington—"Wash" for short—and his big brothers fought mock battles, slashing at each other with wooden swords.

He drew pictures, devoured exciting books, and dreamed of going to sea, much like Daniel Defoe's Robinson Crusoe.

"With what longing eyes would I gaze after [parting ships'] lessening sails and waft myself in imagination to the ends of the earth." W.I. 1818 The Sketch Book

When he was 13 or so, he started going to plays and trying to write his own. But theatergoing took some planning.

Mr. Irving insisted that his family be home by nine P.M. for nightly prayers.

Some nights, Wash would sneak out his window, down a steep rooftop to the yard, to the alley, and back to the theater for the late show. Daring doings—but real adventure was waiting in the wings.

When he was 15, Wash went on his first journey: upriver to Tarrytown, New York, away from New York City's 1798 yellow fever epidemic.

In 1800 and in 1802, on trips to visit his married sisters, he traveled farther up the majestic Hudson to the rugged wilds north of the Mohawk River.

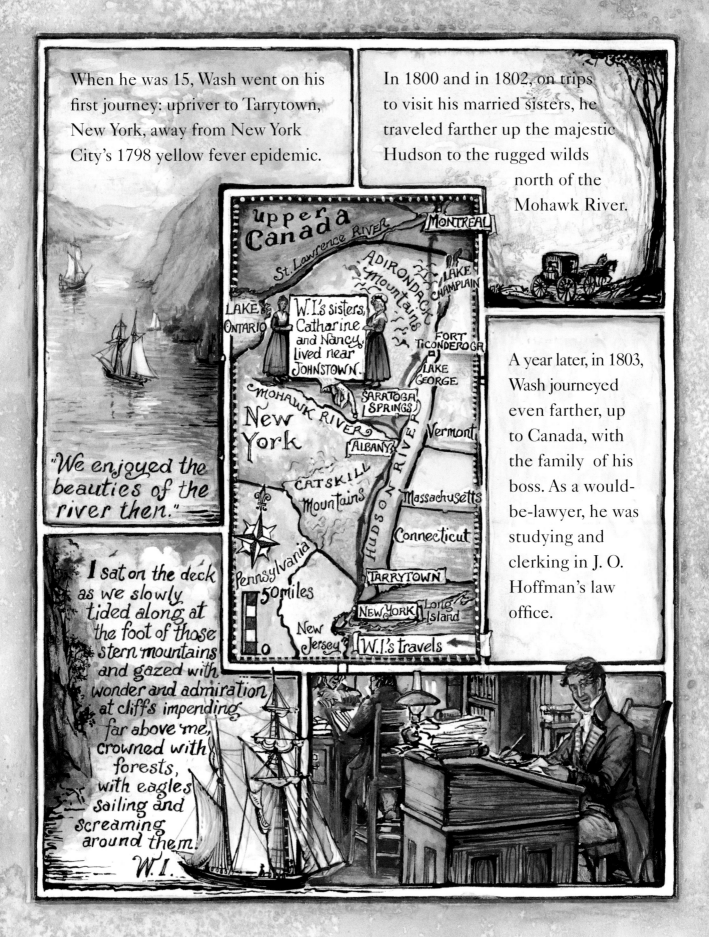

"We enjoyed the beauties of the river then."

A year later, in 1803, Wash journeyed even farther, up to Canada, with the family of his boss. As a would-be-lawyer, he was studying and clerking in J. O. Hoffman's law office.

I sat on the deck as we slowly tided along at the foot of those stern mountains and gazed with wonder and admiration at cliffs impending far above me, crowned with forests, with eagles sailing and screaming around them. W.I.

Map labels:
upper Canada
MONTREAL
St. Lawrence River
ADIRONDACK Mountains
LAKE CHAMPLAIN
LAKE ONTARIO
W. I.'s sisters, Catharine and Nancy, lived near JOHNSTOWN.
FORT TICONDEROGA
LAKE GEORGE
MOHAWK RIVER
SARATOGA SPRINGS
New York
Vermont
ALBANY
HUDSON RIVER
CATSKILL Mountains
Massachusetts
Connecticut
Pennsylvania
TARRYTOWN
50 miles
New Jersey
NEW YORK
Long Island
W.I.'s travels

14

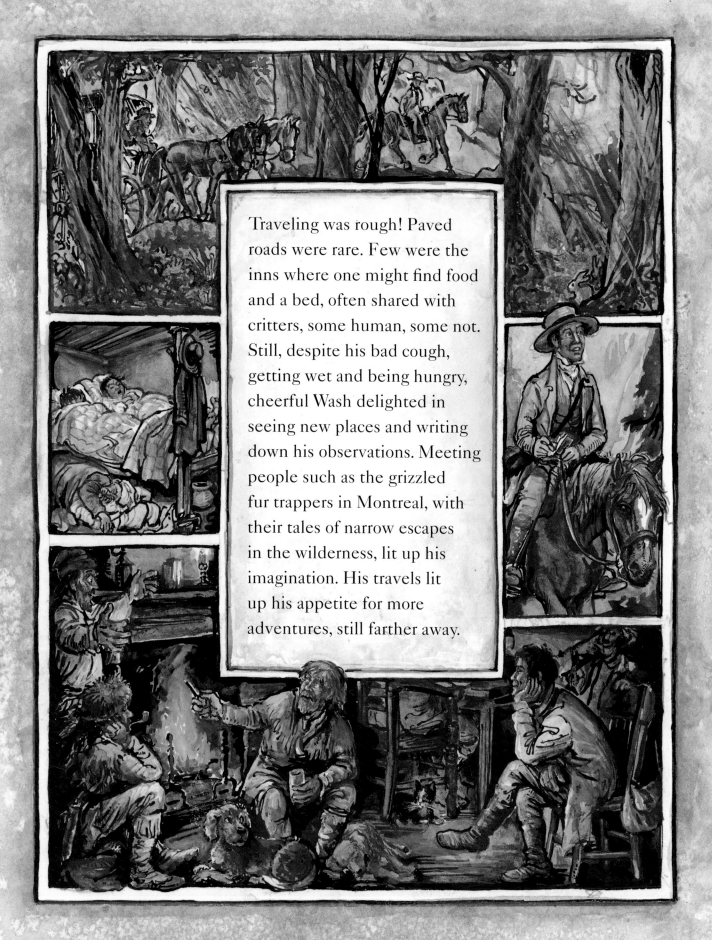

Traveling was rough! Paved roads were rare. Few were the inns where one might find food and a bed, often shared with critters, some human, some not. Still, despite his bad cough, getting wet and being hungry, cheerful Wash delighted in seeing new places and writing down his observations. Meeting people such as the grizzled fur trappers in Montreal, with their tales of narrow escapes in the wilderness, lit up his imagination. His travels lit up his appetite for more adventures, still farther away.

In May 1804, Wash Irving sailed for Europe. His family knew the value of foreign travel, and they hoped that the sea air would make him healthier.

He did indeed feel better by the time he got to France, a nation at war, thanks to its new emperor, Napoleon I. This military genius, who rose to power during the horrific French Revolution (1789–1799), had a huge appetite for conquest. For Wash, traveling in wartime Europe meant difficult border crossings and having to prove that he wasn't a spy. He saw the British fleet commanded by Admiral Horatio Nelson, Napoleon's archenemy, but young Mr. Irving saw no battles on land or sea. He did see pirates, though.

HORATIO NELSON

HMS Victory Flagship of the British fleet

NAPOLEON BONAPARTE

These sea bandits would sail in close, throw hooked ropes onto a ship's deck, scramble aboard, steal from their victims, kidnap them, or toss them overboard. There is little evidence of folks having to "walk the plank." But that would have been of little comfort to Wash when ragged, bearded buccaneers attacked the *Matilda*, the ship he was on, near Italy, in 1804.

"They may be termed banditti of the ocean." W.I.

After some tense hours of tearing around, studying everyone's papers, stealing brandy and such, they left the *Matilda*'s lucky passengers with their lives and bad dreams filled with cutlasses, pistols, daggers, and fierce, dark eyes.

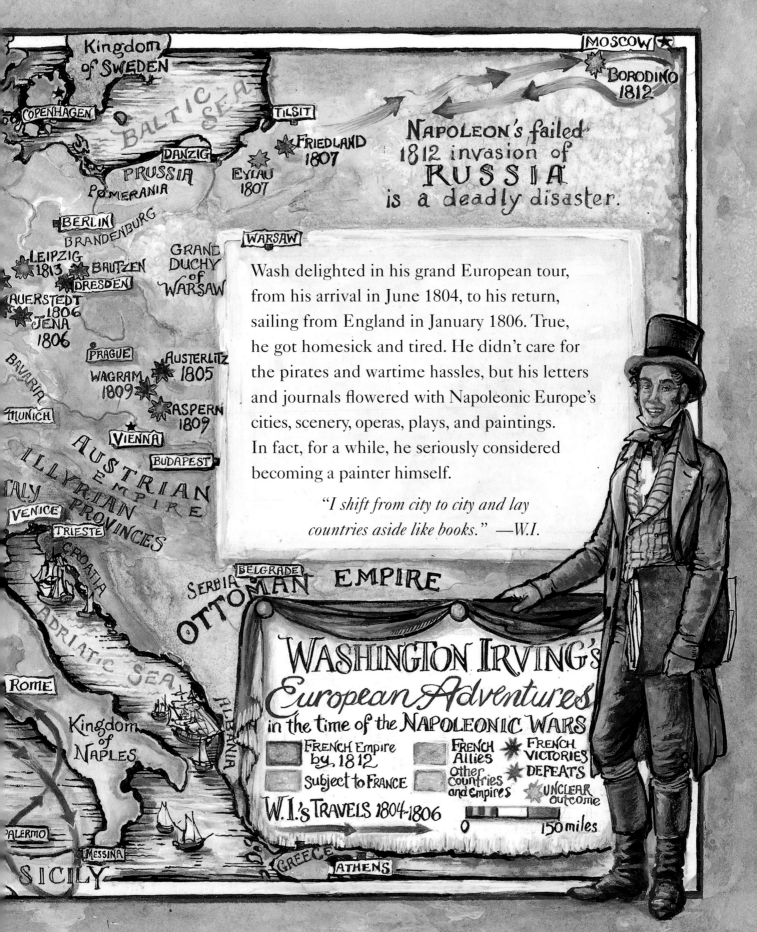

Kingdom of Sweden

MOSCOW ★

BORODINO 1812

COPENHAGEN

BALTIC SEA

TILSIT

FRIEDLAND 1807

Napoleon's failed 1812 invasion of RUSSIA is a deadly disaster.

DANZIG

PRUSSIA

POMERANIA

EYLAU 1807

BERLIN

BRANDENBURG

WARSAW

LEIPZIG 1813

BAUTZEN

DRESDEN

GRAND DUCHY of WARSAW

AUERSTEDT 1806

JENA 1806

PRAGUE

AUSTERLITZ 1805

WAGRAM 1809

ASPERN 1809

BAVARIA

MUNICH

VIENNA

BUDAPEST

ITALY

AUSTRIAN EMPIRE

ILLYRIAN PROVINCES

VENICE

TRIESTE

CROATIA

BELGRADE

SERBIA

OTTOMAN EMPIRE

ADRIATIC SEA

ALBANIA

ROME

Kingdom of NAPLES

PALERMO

MESSINA

SICILY

GREECE

ATHENS

Wash delighted in his grand European tour, from his arrival in June 1804, to his return, sailing from England in January 1806. True, he got homesick and tired. He didn't care for the pirates and wartime hassles, but his letters and journals flowered with Napoleonic Europe's cities, scenery, operas, plays, and paintings. In fact, for a while, he seriously considered becoming a painter himself.

"I shift from city to city and lay countries aside like books." —W.I.

WASHINGTON IRVING'S European Adventures in the time of the NAPOLEONIC WARS

FRENCH Empire by 1812

Subject to FRANCE

FRENCH Allies

Other countries and Empires

FRENCH VICTORIES

DEFEATS

UNCLEAR outcome

W.I.'s TRAVELS 1804-1806

0   150 miles

Back home in New York, Washington took up his old job. Then, having passed the bar exam, newly-minted Lawyer Irving went to Virginia to help an old friend who was in trouble: Aaron Burr. Burr had been Thomas Jefferson's vice president in 1804, when he fought a duel with ex-Secretary of the Treasury, Alexander Hamilton. Hamilton died.

BURR • JEFFERSON • HAMILTON

DUEL!

JULY 11, 1804

"Oh BURR, what hast thou done? Thou hast shooted dead great HAMILTON!" anonymous poem

Now, in 1807, it was said that Burr was a traitor, involved in a murky plot to invade Mexico. In the end, the notorious Burr was found not guilty and he left the country. For his part, Wash went home by way of Washington, D.C., paying a call on President Jefferson.

More fun by far was the time Wash spent talking politics, poetry, and theater with his brothers and friends. He and William and one of their buddies wrote pieces for *Salmagundi*, their magazine.

And he'd begun a grand writing project of his own—that is, when he and Judge Hoffman's daughter weren't sketching and reading poetry together. In time, as she fell ill with tuberculosis, 17-year-old Matilda claimed still more of his attention.

"I was the last one she looked upon." W.I.

"Beautiful and more beautiful," she was to Wash, who'd set his heart on her becoming his bride. But she faded away before his eyes and died on April 26, 1809. Wash Irving plunged himself and his grief into his writing, but he never forgot Matilda Hoffman. And he never married.

W. I.

On December 6, 1809, the public
was offered the chance to buy
copies of *A History of New York*,
by Diedrich Knickerbocker, a
mysterious old gent they'd read
about in the newspaper. Folks so
delighted in his comical telling of
the colonial past and the way he
poked fun at modern politicians that
the book was an instant success—
for Washington Irving, of course.

DIEDRICH KNICKERBOCKER

He made up the author, wrote the book, and made sure it came out on the feast day of Sinterklaas (Saint Nicholas), who was much loved by NY's Dutch colonists. The good saint had always been pictured as a tall, thin bishop riding a white horse—that is, until W.I., in his book, gave us a stout, jolly St. Nick, who rode "over the tops of the trees, in that self-same wagon wherein he brings his yearly presents to children."

SINTERKLAAS

Saint Nicholas

"At this early period was instituted that pious ceremony...of hanging up a stocking on St. Nicholas Eve, which stocking is always found in the morning miraculously filled, for the good St. Nicholas has ever been a great giver of gifts, particularly to children." D.K. (W.I.)

23

In the early 1800s, U.S. ships got no respect. They kept getting raided and tangled in Great Britain's war with France: Bad for international relations, for seafarers, and for merchants like the Irving brothers. If ships couldn't carry goods safely across the Atlantic, their business would be sunk! So Wash went to represent the family enterprise in Washington, D.C. There he met brainy President James Madison, and danced with his popular First Lady, Dolley.

"Mrs. Madison is a fine, portly, buxom dame, who has a smile and a pleasant word for everyone...but as for Jemmy Madison—ah poor Jemmy!—he is but a withered apple-John." W.I. January 13, 1811

She earned lasting fame later on, when U.S. troubles at sea finally sparked another war with the British. Dolley Madison saved official papers, George Washington's portrait, and her pet macaw and escaped from the White House just before the Redcoats set it on fire!

WAR OF 1812

CANADA (British) — QUEBEC
Battle of the THAMES 1813 — MONTREAL
FORT MACKINAC 1812
(TORONTO) YORK 1813 — CHRYSLER'S FARM 1813
DETROIT 1812, 1813
BUFFALO 1813
FORT DEARBORN 1812
LUNDY'S LANE 1813
NEW YORK
RAISIN RIVER 1813
Battle of LAKE ERIE 1813
WASHINGTON 1814
BALTIMORE 1814
BRITISH NAVAL BLOCKADE

UNITED STATES

HORSESHOE BEND 1814

FORT MIMS

Battle of NEW ORLEANS 1815
MOBILE BAY
EAST FLORIDA (Spanish)

American Victories ✱ British Victories ✱ ■ FORTS

As an aide to New York's governor, Colonel Wash Irving didn't see quite so much action in the War of 1812—which, by the way, did not end until 1815, a very big year. The great Napoleon was defeated once and for all at the Battle of Waterloo, in Belgium. And Wash sailed to England. For the next two years, he and his brother Peter tried to save the Irvings' sinking business, but it was no use. So it was that Washington Irving turned to full-time writing.

"IF I indeed have the means within me of establishing a legitimate literary reputation, this is the very period of life most auspicious for it." W.I., in a letter to Ebenezer, March 1, 1819

25

Readers loved *The Sketch Book of Geoffrey Crayon, Gent*, published in two volumes in 1818 and 1819. One of the stories, Rip Van Winkle, was said to have been found in the papers of the late Mr. D. Knickerbocker. Of course, it was Mr. W. Irving himself who totally Americanized a German folktale: In the old colonial times, high in New York's Catskill Mountains, Rip met a silent band of Dutchmen, "dressed in quaint, outlandish fashion," playing at ninepins (bowling). After a sip or two of their beer, he conked out, awoke twenty years later, a snowy old man in a changed world, children grown, the Revolutionary War fought and won.

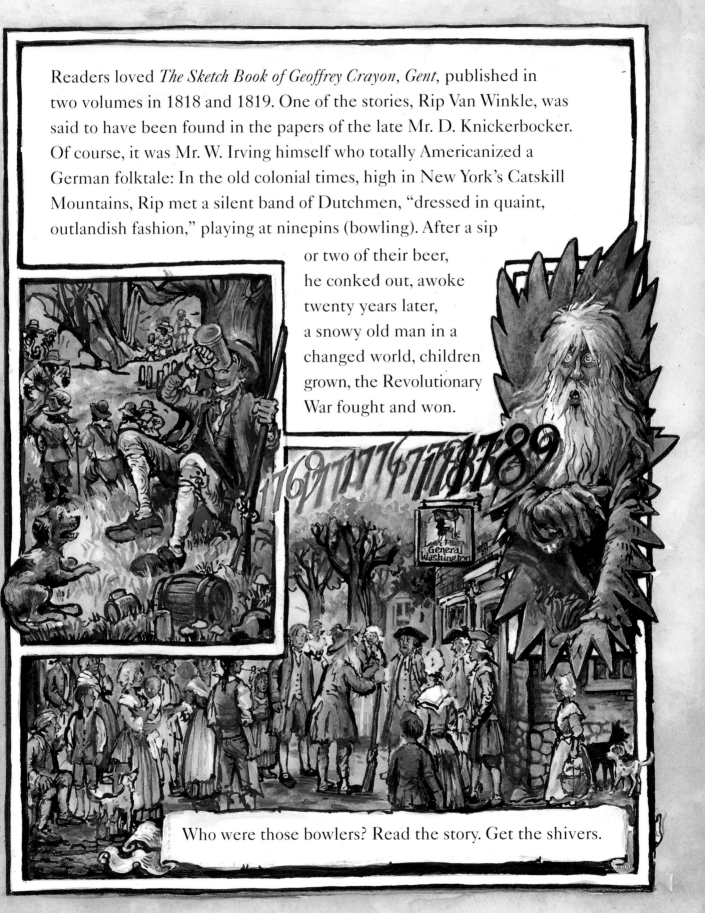

Who were those bowlers? Read the story. Get the shivers.

Sad, funny, and even creepier was "The Legend
of Sleepy Hollow." A ghostly rider was said to gallop through
the Hudson River countryside, seeking his head, which had
been blown off by a cannonball "in some nameless battle in the
Revolutionary War." The main character, nervous, gawky Ichabod
Crane, was no match for the Headless Horseman.

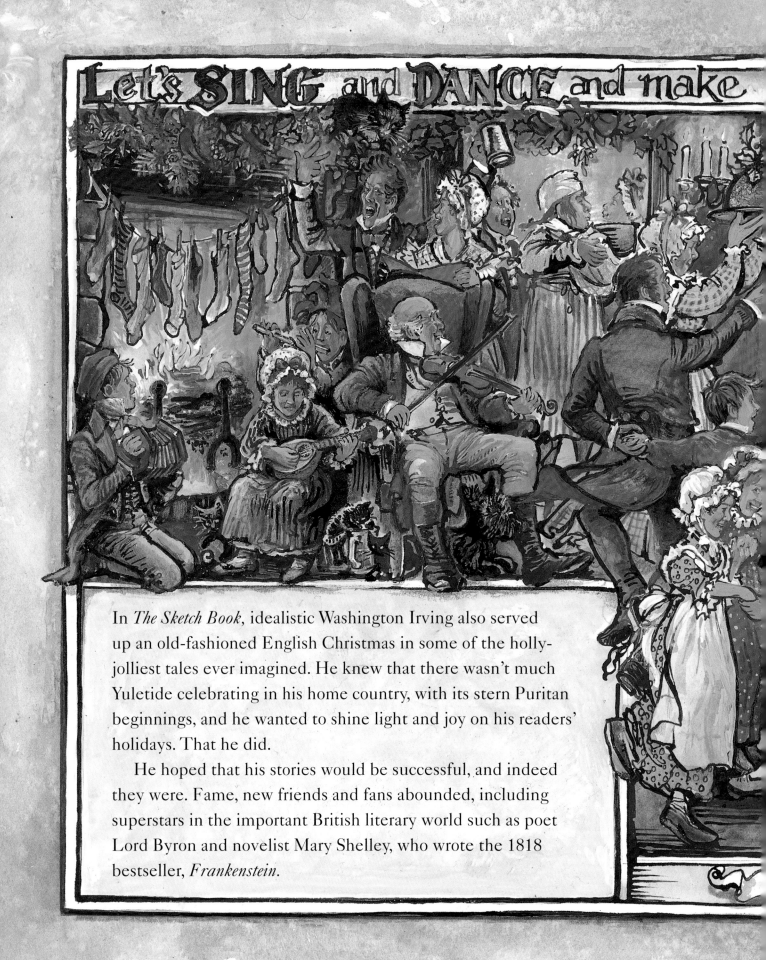

Let's SING and DANCE and make

In *The Sketch Book*, idealistic Washington Irving also served up an old-fashioned English Christmas in some of the holly-jolliest tales ever imagined. He knew that there wasn't much Yuletide celebrating in his home country, with its stern Puritan beginnings, and he wanted to shine light and joy on his readers' holidays. That he did.

He hoped that his stories would be successful, and indeed they were. Fame, new friends and fans abounded, including superstars in the important British literary world such as poet Lord Byron and novelist Mary Shelley, who wrote the 1818 bestseller, *Frankenstein*.

Good CHEER for CHRISTMAS

comes but once a year. anonymous 1652

There is something in the very season of the year that gives a charm to the festivity of CHRISTMAS. W.I.

Washington Irving's European Travels 1817~1832

SCOTLAND
EDINBURGH
W.I. visits Walter Scott, literary star, Summer 1817
SWEDEN
DEN.
EAST PRUSSIA
PRUSSIA
RUSSIAN EMPIRE
WARSAW
POLAND
LIVERPOOL
IRELAND
WALES
ENGLAND
LONDON
AMSTERDAM
ROTTERDAM
ANTWERP
DRESDEN
1822-1823
SOUTHAMPTON
HAVRE
PARIS
MAINZ
FRANKFURT
HEIDELBURG
BAVARIA
PRAGUE
VIENNA
GALICIA
BORDEAUX
STRASBOURG
MUNICH
SALZBURG
AUSTRIAN EMPIRE
HUNGARY
TRANSYLVANIA
FRANCE
SWITZERLAND
SARDINIA
LOMBARDY VENETIA
MODENA
WALLACHIA
OTTOMAN EMPIRE
BOSNIA
SERBIA
PORTUGAL
SPAIN
MADRID
BARCELONA
CORSICA
LUCCA
TUSCANY
PAPAL STATES
ALBANIA
SEVILLE
The Alhambra
VALENCIA
GRANADA 1829
MILAGA
SARDINIA
Kingdom of the Two SICILIES
GREECE

"My fate seems to be to wander, or rather, it is my vocation." W.I.1822

Ferdinand

Isabella

Wash Irving's writing reflected his enthusiasms. As his interests turned to Spain, he became an honorary part of a U.S. diplomatic mission there. He went to study and write about Christopher Columbus, whose explorations were bankrolled by Spain's King Ferdinand and Queen Isabella. In 1492, the brave, bigoted navigator went looking for India, instead found America, and set the long troubles of the "Indians" in motion. But before he sailed, Columbus paid a call on his royal backers down in Granada, Spain, at a fortress known as the Alhambra. So Washington went there, too.

Christopher Columbus

"It is impossible to contemplate this delicious abode and not feel an admiration of the genius and poetical spirit of those who first devised this...paradise." W.I. 1828

The huge, towering, redbrick palace was built by the Moors, Islamic folks from North Africa and Arabia. More than 1,000 years before Wash Irving's lifetime, the Moors invaded Spain, bringing their religion, architecture, and advanced knowledge of math and medicine. For centuries, the Spaniards and the Moors clashed and mingled until Ferdinand and Isabella's forces defeated them in 1492 at the Alhambra, the last Moorish stronghold. Wash put all of this and more in such books as *Tales of the Alhambra*. His admiring readers called it his "Spanish Sketch Book."

"In the evening when I throw by my pen I wander about the old palace until quite late, with nothing but bats and owls to keep me company." W.I.

Washington Irving knew all sorts of important people on both sides of the Atlantic Ocean who realized that he was wise in the ways of the world. So, in 1829, he was asked to work alongside America's ambassador to Great Britain. He accepted, made the long, difficult journey to London and became Secretary Irving of the U.S. diplomatic legation.

He discussed trade and other international goings-on. Being a genial, clever man, Wash made friends for his country. Being a literary adventurer, he wrote and rambled about England;

"I only regret that I had not been left entirely alone, and to dream away life in my own way." W. I. 1829

but being an American at heart, he missed his native land.

"I have been in a tumult of enjoyment ever since my arrival; am pleased with everything and everybody, and as happy as mortal being can be." W.I. 1832

· WASHINGTON IRVING of NEW YORK ·

In time, he resigned his position and sailed west to a hero's welcome home in New York City, on May 21, 1832. But it wasn't long before he was off on fresh adventures. After 17 years abroad, Wash Irving was eager to see as much of his country as he could.

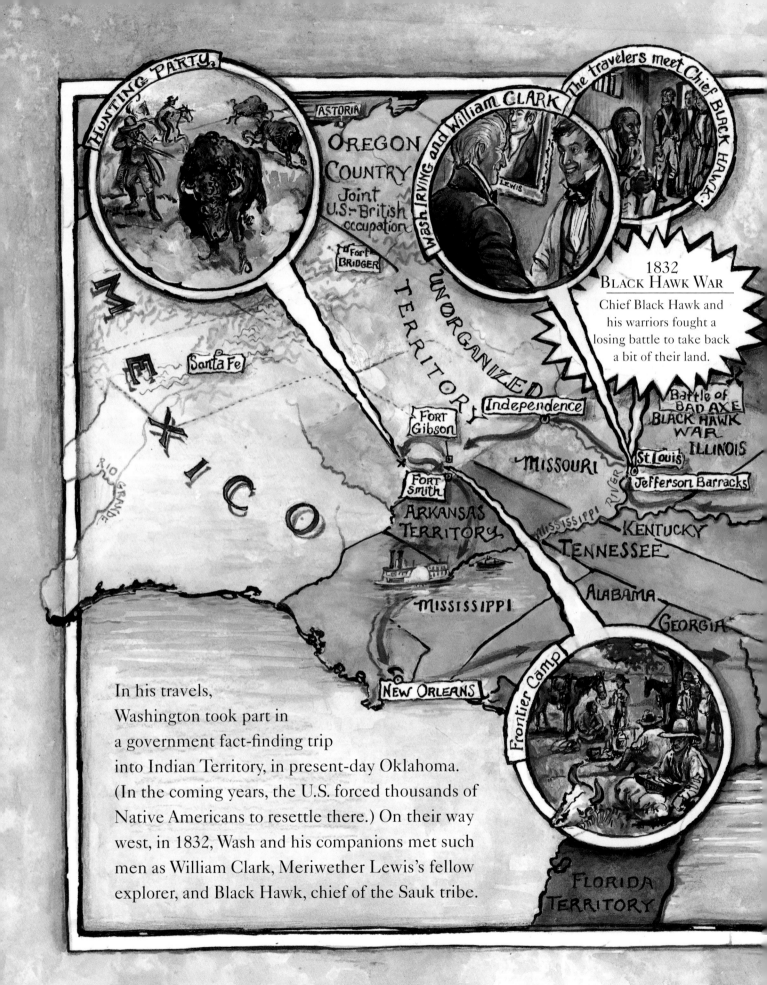

HUNTING PARTY

ASTORIA

OREGON COUNTRY
Joint U.S.-British occupation

Fort BRIDGER

Wash Irving and William CLARK

LEWIS

The travelers meet Chief BLACK HAWK

1832
BLACK HAWK WAR
Chief Black Hawk and his warriors fought a losing battle to take back a bit of their land.

MEXICO

Santa Fe

UNORGANIZED TERRITORY

Independence

Fort Gibson

Fort Smith

ARKANSAS TERRITORY

RIO GRANDE

Battle of BAD AXE
BLACK HAWK WAR
ILLINOIS

St. Louis

Jefferson Barracks

MISSOURI

MISSISSIPPI RIVER

KENTUCKY

TENNESSEE

ALABAMA

GEORGIA

MISSISSIPPI

NEW ORLEANS

Frontier Camp

In his travels, Washington took part in a government fact-finding trip into Indian Territory, in present-day Oklahoma. (In the coming years, the U.S. forced thousands of Native Americans to resettle there.) On their way west, in 1832, Wash and his companions met such men as William Clark, Meriwether Lewis's fellow explorer, and Black Hawk, chief of the Sauk tribe.

FLORIDA TERRITORY

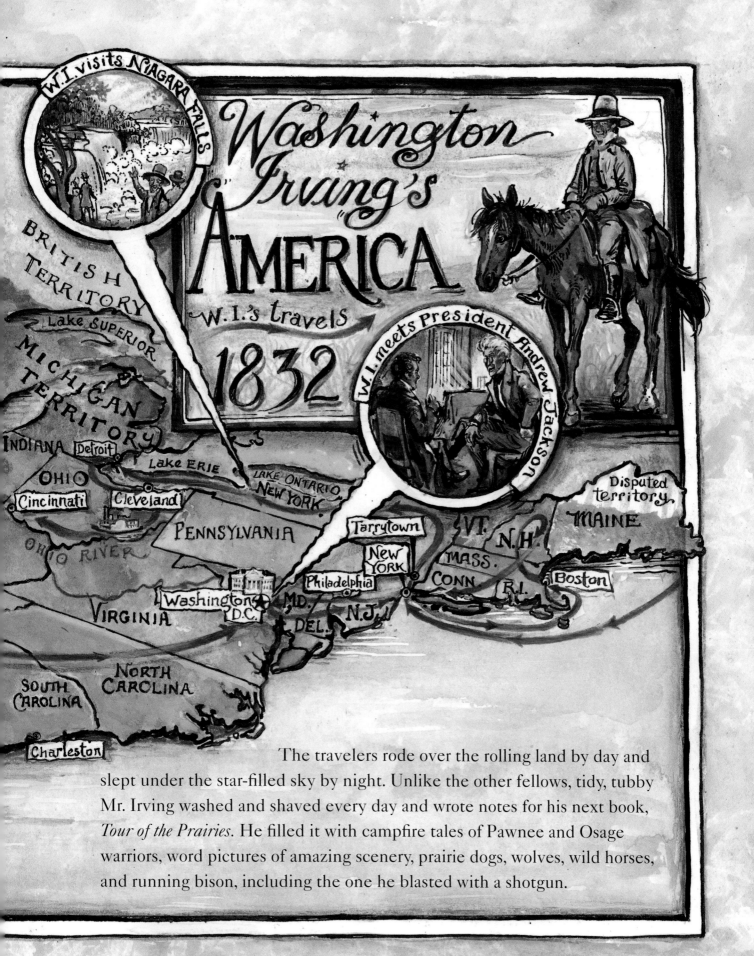

Washington Irving's AMERICA

W.I.'s travels 1832

W.I. visits Niagara Falls

W.I. meets President Andrew Jackson

BRITISH TERRITORY

Lake Superior

MICHIGAN TERRITORY

Indiana · Detroit
OHIO · Lake Erie
Cincinnati · Cleveland
OHIO RIVER
PENNSYLVANIA
Lake Ontario
NEW YORK

Tarrytown
New York
Philadelphia
Washington D.C. · MD.
DEL. · N.J.
VIRGINIA
VT. · N.H.
MASS.
CONN · R.I.
Boston
Disputed territory
MAINE

NORTH CAROLINA
SOUTH CAROLINA
Charleston

The travelers rode over the rolling land by day and slept under the star-filled sky by night. Unlike the other fellows, tidy, tubby Mr. Irving washed and shaved every day and wrote notes for his next book, *Tour of the Prairies.* He filled it with campfire tales of Pawnee and Osage warriors, word pictures of amazing scenery, prairie dogs, wolves, wild horses, and running bison, including the one he blasted with a shotgun.

Wash Irving would write more about men who ventured into the West, such as wealthy John Jacob Astor, a former fur trader. As for the far-traveling author, his thoughts turned to home—a home of his own. In 1835, he bought a cottage built in 1656, near Tarrytown, NY. Craftsmen set to work turning it into the extraordinary house that its artistic owner had in mind, with room for company and family members who would live there, too. Soon fancy old weather vanes perched atop gables, stair-stepped in the Dutch manner. In time, there'd be a tower and a pond. Among the outbuildings was a barn for animals such as Washington's pet pig. He named his pig Fanny and his home Sunnyside.

Tarrytown, N.Y.

When important folks said that the famous Mr. Irving should be mayor of New York, he said no. Secretary of the U.S. Navy? No. U.S. Minister to Spain? Wash would be honored: Yes.

"The only drawback upon all this is the hard trial of tearing myself away from dear little SUNNYSIDE."

W.I. 1842

He left Sunnyside in the care of brother Ebenezer, went to see President John Tyler, and sailed in April 1842.

Once in Europe, he called on Victoria, the popular young British queen,

as well as the unpopular French king Louis Philippe. At last, in August, he presented himself to 12-year-old Princess Isabella, the yet-to-be crowned queen of Spain.

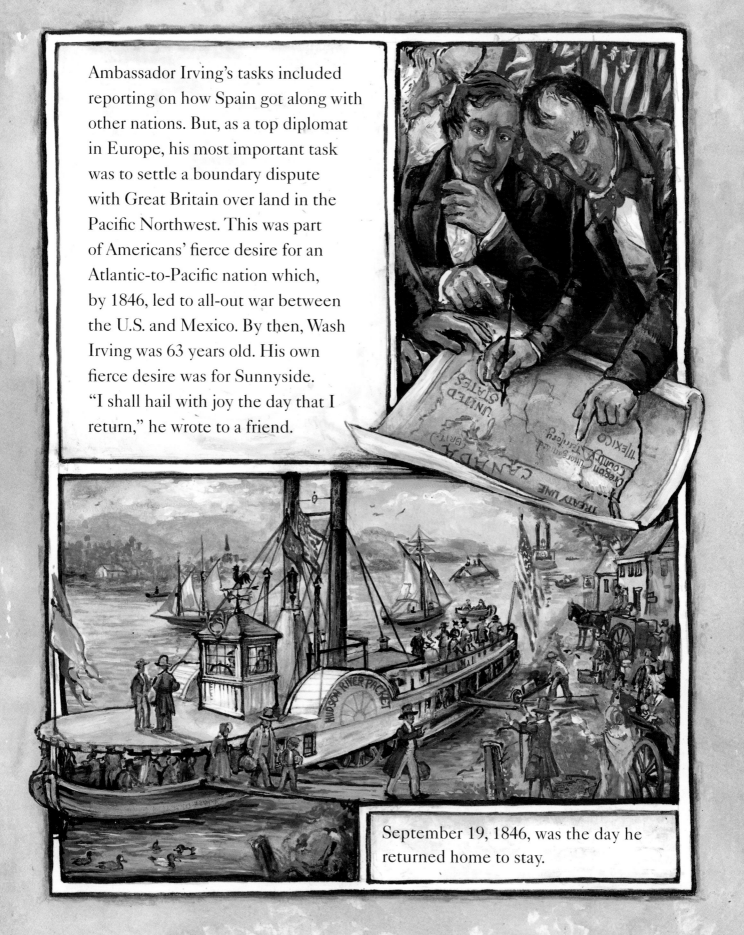

Ambassador Irving's tasks included reporting on how Spain got along with other nations. But, as a top diplomat in Europe, his most important task was to settle a boundary dispute with Great Britain over land in the Pacific Northwest. This was part of Americans' fierce desire for an Atlantic-to-Pacific nation which, by 1846, led to all-out war between the U.S. and Mexico. By then, Wash Irving was 63 years old. His own fierce desire was for Sunnyside. "I shall hail with joy the day that I return," he wrote to a friend.

September 19, 1846, was the day he returned home to stay.

The squire of Sunnyside was happy to stay put, but his restless pen kept on the move. Stories. Letters to friends and fans. A biography of Oliver Goldsmith, an admirable author. A history of Muhammad, the prophet of Islam. Revising earlier writings for new editions. Washington wrote to pay the bills, and he worked hard to make it look easy.

Still, never had he found, so he told a visitor, "any enjoyment equal to sitting at my writing desk, with a clean page, a new theme, and a mind wide awake."

his almost exhausted hour-glass before thee? — hasten then to pursue thy weary task, lest the sands be run ere thou hast finished thy history." DIEDRICH Knickerbocker (W.I.) A HISTORY of New YORK 1809 Is not TIME — relentless TIME! shaking, with palsied hand,

"When I was young my IMAGINATION was always in the advance, picturing out the FUTURE and building CASTLES in the AIR, now MEMORY comes in the place of IMAGINATION and I Look back over the region I have traveled."
Washington Irving
1845

Now, in the last years of his life, the theme he had in mind was the life of George Washington, the tall, calm-faced man he had met when he was six. But that little boy had become a sick old man, short of breath. He needed the help of his nephew (and future biographer), Pierre Munro Irving, to complete the huge task—five volumes! The last chapters of the *Life of Washington* went to the printer just a few months before a heart attack ended the remarkable life of 76-year-old Washington Irving on November 28, 1859.

Church bells chimed in the steeples of New York City. Flags were lowered for the first American author to win serious, worldwide acclaim. He lies buried in the Sleepy Hollow graveyard.

WASHINGTON IRVING
BORN
April 3, 1783
DIED
Nov. 28, 1859

Chronology

April 3, 1783 · Washington Irving (WI) is born to William and Sarah Sanders Irving in NYC.

1802 · WI publishes essays under the name "Jonathan Oldstyle."

May 19, 1804–March 2, 1806 WI's first European travels.

November 21, 1806 · WI barely passes his NY bar examination.

April 26, 1809 · Matilda Hoffman, WI's fiancée, dies.

December 6, 1809 · *A History of New York from the Beginning of the World to the End of the Dutch Dynasty* by Diedrich Knickerbocker.

May 25, 1815 · WI sails to Liverpool, England.

February 2, 1818 · the Irvings' family business goes bankrupt.

1819–1820 · *The Sketch Book of Geoffrey Crayon, Gent.*

1821 · Columbia University awards WI an honorary Master of Arts degree.

1822 · *Bracebridge Hall.* WI lives in Dresden, Germany.

1823 · *Tales of a Traveller*

1826–1829 · WI lives in Madrid, Seville, and Granada, Spain.

1828 · *Life and Voyages of Christopher Columbus*

1829 · *The Conquest of Granada.* WI is appointed Secretary of the U.S. Legation in London, England.

1830 · Royal Society of Literature (London) awards WI its Gold Medal in History.

1831 · *Voyages and Discoveries of the Companions to Columbus*

1832 · *The Alhambra.* He's awarded honorary doctoral degrees from Oxford and Harvard Universities and returns to the U.S.

1835 · *A Tour of the Prairies.* WI purchases Sunnyside, in Tarrytown, NY.

1836 · *Astoria*

1837 · *The Adventures of Captain Bonneville*

1842–1846 · WI is U.S. Minister to Spain.

1848–1851 · WI's revised works are published in 15 volumes.

1849–1850 · *A Book of the Hudson, Oliver Goldsmith, Mahomet, Mahomet and His Successors.*

1855–1859 · *Wolfert's Roost, Life of George Washington* (5 volumes).

November 28, 1859 · WI dies at Sunnyside.

Bibliography

Burstein, Andrew. *The Original Knickerbocker, The Life of Washington Irving.* Cambridge, MA: Basic Books, 2007.

Butler, Joseph T. *Washington Irving's Sunnyside.* Tarrytown, NY: Sleepy Hollow Restorations, 1974.

Caduto, Michael J. and Bruchac, Joseph. *Keepers of the Faith.* Golden, CO: Fulcrum, Inc., 1988.

Dorson, Richard M. *American Folklore.* Chicago: The University of Chicago Press, 1959.

Edmiston, Susan and Cirino, Linda D. *Literary New York, A History and Guide.* Boston: Houghton Mifflin Company, 1976.

Irving, Pierre M. *The Life and Letters of Washington Irving* (4 vol.). New York: G. P. Putnam, 1863.

Jones, Brian Jay. *Washington Irving, An American Original.* New York: Arcade Publishing, 2008.

Tuttleton, James W., ed. *Washington Irving: History, Tales and Sketches.* Cambridge, England: The Library of America, 1983.

Williams, Stanley T. *The Life of Washington Irving.* 2 vols. New York: Oxford University Press, 1935.

Places to Visit

• Washington Irving's life began at 131 William Street, between Fulton Street and John Street in New York City

•Directions to his final resting place can be found, along with other cool info, at www.sleepyhollowcemetery.org

•You may have a guided tour of Sunnyside:

Washington Irving's Sunnyside
89 West Sunnyside Lane
Tarrytown, NY 10591
Phone: 914-591-8763

For More Information

www.hudsonvalley.org/education/Background/abt_irving/abt_irving.html

Dedication:
This book is affectionately dedicated to Betsy Polivy, lover of books, and to Natalie Kinsey Warnock, with whom I visited Sunnyside.

Acknowledgment:
I am most grateful for the hospitality of Sunnyside's Site Director, Ms. Dina Rose Friedman.

Library of Congress Cataloging-in-Publication Data

Harness, Cheryl.
  The literary adventures of Washington Irving : American storyteller / by Cheryl Harness.
     p. cm.
  Includes bibliographical references.
  ISBN 978-1-4263-0438-5 (alk. paper) -- ISBN 978-1-4263-0439-2 (lib. bdg . : alk. paper)
  1. Irving, Washington, 1783-1859--Juvenile literature. 2. Authors, American--19th century--Biography--Juvenile literature. I. Title.
  PS2081.H34 2008
  818'.209--dc22
  [B]
                                    2008024975

Founded in 1888, the National Geographic Society is one of the largest nonprofit scientific and educational organizations in the world. It reaches more than 285 million people worldwide each month through its official journal, NATIONAL GEOGRAPHIC, and its four other magazines; the National Geographic Channel; television documentaries; radio programs; films; books; videos and DVDs; maps; and interactive media. National Geographic has funded more than 8,000 scientific research projects and supports an education program combating geographic illiteracy.

For more information, please call 1-800-NGS LINE (647-5463) or write to the following address:

National Geographic Society
1145 17th Street N.W., Washington, D.C. 20036-4688 U.S.A.

Visit us online at
www.nationalgeographic.com/books

Printed in Canada